DAVID AUBURN

LOST LAKE

David Auburn was born in Chicago and grew up in Ohio and Arkansas. He lives in New York City with his wife and two daughters.

LOST
LAKE

LOST LAKE

A PLAY BY

DAVID AUBURN

FARRAR, STRAUS AND GIROUX

NEW YORK

Farrar, Straus and Giroux
18 West 18th Street, New York 10011

Library of Congress Cataloging-in-Publication Data
Auburn, David, 1969–
    Lost lake : a play / David Auburn. — First edition.
        pages ;   cm
    ISBN 978-0-86547-836-7 (softcover) — ISBN 978-0-374-71414-7 (ebook)
    1. Friendship—Drama.   2. Man-woman relationships—Drama.   I. Title.

PS3551.U28 L67 2015
812'.54—dc23   2015003936

Designed by Abby Kagan

Our books may be purchased in bulk for promotional, educational, or business use.
Please contact your local bookseller or the Macmillan Corporate and Premium
Sales Department at 1-800-221-7945, extension 5442, or by e-mail at
MacmillanSpecialMarkets@macmillan.com.

www.fsgbooks.com
www.twitter.com/fsgbooks • www.facebook.com/fsgbooks

1   3   5   7   9   10   8   6   4   2

TO FRAN

LOST
LAKE

Lost Lake was developed during a residency at the Eugene O'Neill Theater Center's National Playwrights Conference in 2013. Preston Whiteway, executive director; Wendy C. Goldberg, artistic director.

Produced as part of the inaugural season of the Sullivan Project at Illinois Theatre, University of Illinois at Urbana-Champaign, February 2014. Daniel Sullivan, artistic director; Jeffrey Eric Jenkins, producer.

Originally produced by the Manhattan Theatre Club. Lynne Meadow, artistic director; Barry Grove, executive producer. The first performance was on November 11, 2014.

VERONICA	Tracie Thoms
HOGAN	John Hawkes

Director	Daniel Sullivan
Scenic Design	J. Michael Griggs
Lighting Design	Robert Perry
Costume Design	Jess Goldstein
Original Music and Sound Design	Fitz Patton
Movement Consultant	Thomas Schall
Production Stage Manager	David Sugarman
Stage Manager	Jeff Brancato
Casting	Caparelliotis Casting

SCENE 1

The main room of a dilapidated lakeside cabin.

    VERONICA, *a black woman in her thirties wearing a winter coat, looking around.* HOGAN, *a disheveled white man in his fifties, with her.*

HOGAN: So what do you think?

VERONICA: It looks all right.

(*Beat.*)

HOGAN: I know it's cold now. July–August you won't have to worry about that.

VERONICA: Of course.

HOGAN: Though the last couple weeks of August nights can get cool again, you might want to bring some extra blankets for the kids.

VERONICA: Uh-huh.

(*Beat.*)

HOGAN: How many kids?

VERONICA: Two. Maybe three—the older one, my girl, wants to bring a friend. I haven't decided about that. It may just be her and her brother.

HOGAN: They identical?

VERONICA: What? No.

HOGAN: They are twins, you said.

VERONICA: No. They're two years apart. Boy and girl.

HOGAN: I don't know why I thought they were twins.

VERONICA: No. They're just . . . regular.

(*Beat.*)

HOGAN: There's only one bed in the second room.

VERONICA: That's all right. They can double up.

HOGAN: It's pretty small. I might have a trundle I can get for you.

VERONICA: Oh no, that's fine. One of them can sleep with me if we have to.

HOGAN: Your husband won't mind?

VERONICA: It's just me.

HOGAN: Oh. Sorry.

VERONICA: No. But maybe an extra bed would be—

HOGAN: No problem. I can call my brother, see if I can borrow his trundle. But if the third kid comes—

VERONICA: I think I'm gonna have to tell my little girl that isn't happening.

HOGAN: No, it'll still work. You put one in the single, one on the trundle, and one on the couch in a sleeping bag or whatever. You'd have to bring up some extra linens is all.

VERONICA: We'll figure that out.

HOGAN: She wants to bring a friend, let her. They'll have a ball.

VERONICA: We'll see.

(*Beat.*)

HOGAN: Pretty gorgeous out there, huh? Even this time of year.

VERONICA: Yes, it is.

HOGAN: The dock will be fixed by June. It's almost done now. We finally got around to it.

VERONICA: The dock?

HOGAN: Yeah.

VERONICA: Is there some kind of boat?

HOGAN: Swimming dock.

VERONICA: Oh. Yes.

HOGAN: See out there?

VERONICA: Yes. It's pretty far out.

HOGAN: Nah. It's an easy swim. There's usually a diving board. That'll get put back on. I'm gonna paint the deck a nice fire-engine red after I get the fifteen years of Canada goose shit scrubbed off. You'll see the geese, they shit on everything.

VERONICA: You're doing the work?

HOGAN: I was the low bid.

VERONICA: I see.

HOGAN: Homeowners' association's been putting it off for years. Last summer a woman put her foot through a rotten plank. Had to go to the emergency room to get the splinters out. Finally I said, Look, give me fifteen hundred bucks, I'll have it ready by Memorial Day. I'm going to put in a second diving platform higher up. It's gonna be great. I made some sketches. It'll just be stationary but you'll still have the springboard on the opposite side. You'll never get your kids off it.

VERONICA: They don't really swim.

HOGAN: Why not?

VERONICA: City kids.

HOGAN: That's not good. They need to learn.

VERONICA: That's one of the reasons we wanted to be up here.

HOGAN: It's a life skill. You should get them lessons at the Y or someplace now. That way when they get up here they're ready.

VERONICA: I don't know if we have time for that.

HOGAN: It's only March. You got four months.

VERONICA: Well, we'll see.

HOGAN: Don't let them go to the dock unless you're sure they can manage it.

VERONICA: Of course not.

HOGAN: Now, there is a canoe I'll get out for you, which will require some bailing but it's more or less seaworthy, and I think two life jackets. But I believe only one paddle. I'll check the garage. If I can't find another one I'll ask my brother. But you'd still need a third life jacket if your little girl brings her friend. Or if you need it. Do you swim?

VERONICA: Yes.

HOGAN: Because some . . . city people don't.

VERONICA: I do.

HOGAN: Okay then. Any other questions?

VERONICA: No. I think . . .

(*Beat. She looks around. Swallows her doubts.*)

All right. Let's do it.

HOGAN: Great. You're really gonna enjoy it here.

VERONICA: I hope so.

HOGAN: You will.

VERONICA: So how should we—how do you like to do this?

HOGAN: Well, we talked about the total in the e-mail, that still works for you?

VERONICA: Yes.

HOGAN: So now I guess maybe just a deposit. To hold the rental.

VERONICA: All right.

HOGAN: What if we say half now and then half when you get here. And add maybe five hundred on to the front end as a damage deposit, that I'll refund at the end if everything's shipshape.

VERONICA: So you're saying half the total rental plus five hundred now?

HOGAN: Yes. And you'll get the five hundred back at the end of the summer.

VERONICA: Unless there's damage.

HOGAN: There won't be. I'll put away anything fragile. There's nothing much you can hurt around here anyway even with kids.

VERONICA: So maybe we don't need to do the damage deposit? I'm just—

HOGAN: It's pretty standard.

VERONICA: I'm just wondering if maybe—half plus the five hundred now seems like a lot.

HOGAN: Uh-huh.

VERONICA: I mean I could do half and half, but then maybe

I'd ask you to waive the damage deposit, given that everything around here already looks pretty . . . broken in.

HOGAN: I just thought if something got damaged, I don't even know what—

VERONICA: Uh-huh.

HOGAN: It'd be easier if it's already dealt with, so to speak, rather than negotiate it later—

VERONICA: No, I understand, but maybe then a better way to do the rent would be a third now, a third I can send you let's say in June, and then a third when we come up.

HOGAN: And we'd still do the damage deposit.

VERONICA: Yes. But maybe spread out over the first two payments.

HOGAN: Two fifty, two fifty.

VERONICA: Yes.

HOGAN: Third payment when you get here.

VERONICA: Yes.

(*Beat.*)

HOGAN: Deal!

VERONICA: Okay. Thank you.

HOGAN: Thank you. You're a real wily negotiator, huh?

VERONICA: I don't know about that.

HOGAN: No, I like it! So all right. Any other questions?

VERONICA: Do you have Internet?

HOGAN: No. That would require a dish and it's just not worth it to me. If I need to check my e-mail I drive into town to the library. Cell phone service is spotty. If you stand by the window and kind of elevate yourself a little bit and hold your phone out at about a forty-five-degree angle sometimes a signal can be had—I don't even bother usually, I use the landline for calls at the house and the library for Internet, like I said.

VERONICA: I will need to get online a few times for work. How far is the library?

HOGAN: Ten minutes. It's only open three days a week but you don't even have to go in. When it's closed you can park outside with your laptop. People do it all the time. Oh—you'll need a car. I mean once you get up here. But you saw that.

VERONICA: I'll rent a car for the week.

HOGAN: You got that budgeted in.

VERONICA: Yes.

HOGAN: Well, great, so everything is settled. What sort of work do you do, you don't mind my asking?

VERONICA: I'm a nurse practitioner.

HOGAN: A nurse, huh?

VERONICA: Practitioner, yes.

HOGAN: Which means what?

VERONICA: I can prescribe certain medications, perform certain procedures.

HOGAN: Turn your head and cough, that sort of thing?

VERONICA: I'm sorry?

HOGAN: Sort of halfway to a doctor in other words.

VERONICA: Sort of.

HOGAN: Well, that sounds good.

(*Beat.*)

So, right—if you need to stay in touch with your office or hospital or whatever—

VERONICA: Hospital.

HOGAN: —just give them this number the week you're here. We did say a week, didn't we?

VERONICA: The third week in August.

HOGAN: The last week's available too. Stay till Labor Day.

VERONICA: I have to work.

HOGAN: You only get one week of vacation?

VERONICA: That's all I've been able to arrange.

HOGAN: Then you really should get those kids swimming before they get up here.

VERONICA: Maybe. We'll see.

HOGAN: They'll spend the whole week watching other kids dive off the dock.

VERONICA: We'll manage.

HOGAN: Well, if you change your mind the rest of August is available.

VERONICA: Thank you, but I don't think we'll be able to do that.

(*Beat. She looks at an old hockey stick propped against the wall.*)

HOGAN: I'll get all that stuff out of here before you come, naturally, pack up my clothes and so forth, the drawers will be free. When are you heading back to the city?

VERONICA: (*Takes out a bus schedule.*) I think I can make the three-thirty bus.

HOGAN: Today.

VERONICA: Yes. If you could drop me back in front of the movie theater.

HOGAN: Didn't you just come up this morning?

VERONICA: I wanted to make sure I saw the place before—

HOGAN: No, that's wise. Picking something off the Internet,

who the hell knows what you're going to get? If the pictures they put up are even real. Or the descriptions. The way people exaggerate, you do have to watch out.

VERONICA: Well, you certainly didn't exaggerate.

HOGAN: I said "rustic." That's what you're looking for, isn't it?

VERONICA: Yes.

HOGAN: I'll fix that shutter before you come up. And the dock will be done like I said. And I don't know if you looked in the shower but I'll get that section of ceiling patched and the wall repainted, I've been meaning to borrow some paint from my brother—he has a beautiful robin's-egg blue from when he did his bathrooms. I just need a free weekend.

VERONICA: I definitely would appreciate any . . .

HOGAN: Little improvements—

VERONICA: Yes—you plan to do. The kitchen seems fine.

HOGAN: Don't use the two front burners on the stove, they only work on high and then they smoke. Those I doubt I'll be able to get to—

VERONICA: Did you say you'll be moving your clothes out of here?

HOGAN: Oh, sure. I'll get all the drawers clear for you.

VERONICA: You live here now.

HOGAN: Yes. But I'll get everything cleared out.
    What?

VERONICA: Nothing. Sorry. I suppose I thought this was just a summer place.

HOGAN: It is but lately I've been a full-timer. A couple space heaters and you can get through a winter if it stays mild like it has this year. It's not so bad.

The lake used to freeze over sometimes, believe it or not. We played hockey out there when we were kids. That doesn't happen hardly ever anymore, the winters are so mild now. That's a collector's item. Big hockey fan. You?

VERONICA: Where will you go when we're renting?

HOGAN: My brother's. He's only about forty-five minutes away. So I can be here quickly if anything comes up.

VERONICA: I hate to kick you out of your own house.

HOGAN: Are you kidding? You're doing me a favor. I wish you'd do me a bigger favor and rent all summer.

VERONICA: Your brother'd take you for the whole summer?

HOGAN: That's a good point.

(*Beat.*)

VERONICA: Well, Mr. . . . Hogan?

HOGAN: Yes. Terry.

VERONICA: Let me get you that deposit.

(*She writes a check. She gives it to him.*)

HOGAN: Thank you. (*Looks at it.*) Veronica.

VERONICA: Okay.

(*They shake hands. Beat.*)

I'd better get to that bus stop.

Fade.

SCENE 2

August. Sound of kids playing outside. HOGAN *lets himself into the cabin. It has been straightened up. He notices a large library book. He picks it up, flips through it.*

    VERONICA *enters. Summer clothes.*

VERONICA: You got my messages.

HOGAN: Why I'm here.

VERONICA: Well, good.

HOGAN: Sorry about the delay. My phone died and I couldn't find the charger!

    You a birder?

VERONICA: No.

(*He shows her the book. It's a* Field Guide to North American Birds.)

Oh. No, that's just for my son. He's into birds and wildlife right now, he's always asking their names, so.

HOGAN: How old is he?

VERONICA: Seven.

HOGAN: Wow. Is he some kind of genius?

VERONICA: No.

HOGAN: Pretty heavy reading for a seven-year-old, isn't it? I mean this is like a hard-core scientific text.

VERONICA: It's just in case he wants to look up one of the names. It's what the library had.

HOGAN: Oh. Okay.

(*Beat. She begins setting out lunch.*)

They're having a good time looks like. You got them some lessons?

VERONICA: Yes.

HOGAN: Where'd you get the inner tubes?

VERONICA: I bought them in town.

HOGAN: Great idea.

You know, I taught my own kid to swim out there. She could dive like a porpoise. You should have seen her go off the springboard. Fearless. She always asked, Why isn't there a high platform? There should be a high-dive.

She was right. That's one of the reasons I volunteered to do the dock. You think I was gonna make a profit on that? Forget it. The lumber alone . . .

She's with her mom now. In Florida. But we're still real close. We e-mail . . .

VERONICA: Uh-huh. So look, if you could do something about the hot water I'd appreciate it.

HOGAN: I'll see what I can do.

VERONICA: All right then.

(*Beat.*)

HOGAN: You know, even if they've had a few lessons if you're gonna be in here maybe you should put some water wings on them.

VERONICA: I told them how far in they are allowed to go, and my children do what they're told.

And they had ten lessons. A friend of mine who does physical therapy let us use the pool where she works after hours. I taught them myself.

HOGAN: Okay, great.

VERONICA: You said back in March that the dock would be ready for the summer.

HOGAN: I know.

VERONICA: You said it'd be painted. There'd be a diving board. There's no diving board. There's hardly any dock. Half the planks are gone.

HOGAN: I know it's not ideal.

VERONICA: It's dangerous. My daughter's friend went out the first day, she nearly put her hand through a nail sticking right out of the side. I would have had to get her a tetanus shot. I had to ban them from the dock.

HOGAN: The inner tubes were a good idea.

VERONICA: Four inner tubes from the Kmart duct-taped together are a pretty poor substitute for a swimming dock. And it's sixty dollars I didn't plan to spend.

HOGAN: It's nice your little girl's friend could come up at least.

VERONICA: Mr. Hogan. I think you should reimburse me.

(*He says nothing.*)

You said the dock would be repaired; it isn't. We've been up here three days with no hot water. You did not provide the trundle bed you promised. I've had two nine-year-olds sleeping on a twin bed. You know I saw the place, I wasn't expecting the Four Seasons, but—

HOGAN: I fixed the shutter.

VERONICA: What shutter?

HOGAN: That one, that was off its hinge.

VERONICA: It's ornamental. What do I care about that? This is my vacation. It's been very frustrating.

HOGAN: I understand.

VERONICA: I hope so.

HOGAN: I'm gonna take a look at the water heater right now. I'm sure I can get it going. It's probably just the pilot light.

VERONICA: It's not the pilot light. I know how to check a pilot light. You've got some other problem.

HOGAN: I'll take a look at it right away.

VERONICA: Thank you.

HOGAN: Is there anything else?

VERONICA: You mean besides the dock, the bed, the hot water, the disconnected phone, and the dead tree branch over the walkway looks like it's about to fall and smash in one of my children's skulls any second?

HOGAN: I was not aware about the phone.

VERONICA: I had to use my cell phone. You were right about one thing, you got to be a circus acrobat to get a signal in this place. You know what? I really think it's only fair you consider refunding a portion of my rental fee.

HOGAN: You haven't had a good time?

VERONICA: We have had—we have managed to enjoy ourselves so far, but—

HOGAN: The weather's been gorgeous.

VERONICA: It rained all day yesterday.

HOGAN: Besides that.

VERONICA: I made a decision not to let some of these disappointments ruin my vacation, but—

HOGAN: That's the right attitude. And you know what? Kids don't care. Give them a little water to splash around in they're happy forever.

VERONICA: Yes, but I would like to be able to give them a hot bath afterward. I'd like to be able to take a bath. Call me greedy.

HOGAN: I don't think you're greedy.

VERONICA: Thank you.

HOGAN: But I never did get your third payment.

(*Beat.*)

The last third we agreed you would give me when you arrived.

VERONICA: I know.

HOGAN: Do you have it?

VERONICA: Are you seriously asking for it now?

HOGAN: If you don't mind. We can get that straight and then we can deal with any other issues.

VERONICA: You got it backwards. I think we should deal with this first.

HOGAN: You mean the refund.

VERONICA: I don't need a full refund. We're here now, we're going to stay out the week.

HOGAN: What do you want?

VERONICA: I think you ought to refund, let's say three days' rent.

HOGAN: Uh-huh.

VERONICA: Assuming you can get everything else working. Not the dock of course, I can see that's a lost cause.

HOGAN: There were structural problems with the dock I didn't anticipate.

VERONICA: Uh-huh.

HOGAN: I thought it was just the decking needed replacement. But it was one of the pilings too. They're sunk into concrete under the lake bed. This is a man-made lake. They probably did it before the lake was filled. So they had it easier. I'm not a Navy SEAL. I can't replace a piling that's sunk in four feet of concrete under fifteen feet of water.

VERONICA: Maybe you should have figured that out before you took the job.

HOGAN: Right, that is exactly what the homeowners' association said. Or rather their attorney, which is why I am being sued. Which is why I can't refund your money even if I'd like to. Which I would.

VERONICA: Well, I'm sorry about that.

HOGAN: It is a huge pain in the ass.

VERONICA: But it's not my problem.

(*Beat.*)

HOGAN: I hate to argue about money.

VERONICA: Mr. Hogan, I'm about to give my kids lunch here—

HOGAN: What are you having?

VERONICA: Sandwiches. So I—

HOGAN: What kind?

VERONICA: I got baloney and peanut butter and jelly. Why? Do you want one?

HOGAN: Sure. I haven't eaten.

VERONICA: Okay, let me make myself clearer. I don't exactly feel like giving you lunch right now. I would like to resolve this.

HOGAN: Look, what do you expect me to do? We said twelve hundred for the week. Now, that is not a lot of money for a two-bedroom rental on a lake in this area two weeks before Labor Day. Now you want three days back. That's what, about five hundred bucks?

VERONICA: More like six.

HOGAN: Okay, whatever. I'm gonna deal with your hot water problem. I really don't see how a few days of cold showers, which is good for the circulation by the way—you're a nurse, you should know that—could be worth— How much did you say you wanted?

VERONICA: Six hundred.

HOGAN: But you still owe *me* four hundred. Don't you? Minus whatever you paid for the inner tubes.

VERONICA: Forget the inner tubes. I bought them, that's done.

HOGAN: No, I'll reimburse you for those, I don't have a problem with that. I know you're especially upset about the inner tubes.

VERONICA: I don't care about the damn inner tubes. I care about three days with no hot water.

HOGAN: But you haven't paid rent for those three days!

VERONICA: I—

HOGAN: So why not just pay it?

VERONICA: Because this house is shabby! All right? It's a shabby mess. I had to spend the whole first night cleaning. There's more bugs in this damn house than in my apartment in New York City.

HOGAN: You're in nature, you're not in the goddamn city.

VERONICA: Oh, they're better bugs, is that what you're saying?

HOGAN: If you were expecting an insect-free cabin in the woods I can't help you, that's all, I don't think we have anything to talk about.

VERONICA: And I can't sleep up here. I'm out here in the woods all by myself a million miles from nowhere with three little children, I can't believe how creepy it is at night with the crickets and the frogs and hoot-owls and I don't know what.

HOGAN: Well, I'm sorry but that's what you paid for. Or partially paid for.

VERONICA: Okay, look. Just give me two hundred.

HOGAN: How did you get to two hundred now?

VERONICA: Because! Six hundred you owe me for the three days minus the last third of the rent, the difference is—

HOGAN: All right, all right, all right, the hell with it.

(*He takes out his wallet.*)

I got thirty-eight dollars on me, which is all the cash I've got until my disability comes in Friday. Take it. Go on. Take it.

VERONICA: I don't want your last thirty-eight dollars.

HOGAN: Take it. It's fine. My brother'll tide me over. If Debbie lets him.

VERONICA: Debbie?

HOGAN: His wife. We don't get along.

VERONICA: I can't imagine.

HOGAN: She is not an easygoing person. I like a relaxed atmosphere. I don't like a lot of tension.

VERONICA: Who does?

HOGAN: Debbie. I think she feeds on it.

VERONICA: Mr. Hogan—

HOGAN: No. You keep the cash. That's honestly the best I can do right now. Just make sure your kids stay away from the dock and the stove, all right? Last thing I need is another lawsuit.

(*Beat.*)

VERONICA: You got a lawyer?

HOGAN: Sort of.

VERONICA: What do you mean sort of?

HOGAN: Debbie is a lawyer. A pretty good one, apparently. I've asked her to take my case pro bono. She says she's "considering" it. Isn't that sweet of her? I've got to hope she says yes. If she doesn't I'm done. I'll have to sell this place. I mean I probably have to sell it anyway. The homeowners' association will get something. It's just a question of how dry they can squeeze me. These people on the homeowners' association are not local people. I'm unusual, see. Most of them come up from the fucking city—sorry, but they are the kind of people who are not happy unless they're suing somebody. You want to know the real bitch of it? I'm a member of the homeowners' association! This was my dad's cabin. I was on the board even for a while in the nineties. So it's like I'm suing myself. It's like if I lose I got to go bankrupt trying to pay damages to myself!

VERONICA: No, it's not like that at all.

HOGAN: Anyway, not your problem.

(*At the window.*)

You know, they're really swimming out there.

VERONICA: They better not be swimming.

(*She looks.*)

Hey!

(*She goes outside.*)

HOGAN: Yeah, I would say something about that.

VERONICA: (*Outside.*) Hey! The three of you! I *said* I do not want you out farther than up to your belly buttons! Come on out. Come up on the beach now. *Thank* you!

Just get dried off now. I'm gonna be out there with your lunch in one minute!

(*She comes back in.*)

HOGAN: Kids.

VERONICA: (*Frustrated sound.*)

HOGAN: What'd you end up doing yesterday?

VERONICA: What?

HOGAN: While it was raining.

VERONICA: Nothing. Took them bowling.

HOGAN: Hey. Putnam Lanes? In town?

VERONICA: I guess so. Yes.

HOGAN: I love that place. I haven't been there in years. You still have to keep score yourself or do they have those automatic scorekeepers now?

VERONICA: It's automatic. On screens.

HOGAN: That's too bad. That's a shame. A screen doing it all for you. I used to like taking home the score sheets. And you got those little stubby pencils . . . Remember?

VERONICA: Bowling was not a big part of my childhood.

HOGAN: Putnam Lanes. Can't beat that for keeping kids happy. I used to take my daughter there. I remember she was maybe eight or nine and she'd pick out an eight-pound ball— this little girl!—and stride right up the lane to the line and roll two or three strikes a game, and then write the little X's in the box herself and add up her own score. We probably did that once a month. She's very (*taps his head*). She's going to Columbia University in the fall. Did I tell you that? Full scholarship. Her mom just let me know. A little late, seeing as how she got in in April, I would have appreciated a word then, but— Anyway. I'm proud, I can't deny it. It's supposed to be a hell of a school. It's in your neck of the woods, isn't it?

VERONICA: Sort of.

HOGAN: Maybe I'll drive down there in the fall, check it out. I haven't been down to the city in a long time. Not since everybody had those "no radio" signs on their car windows. They don't do that anymore, do they?

VERONICA: No.

HOGAN: I'd like to see her play. She's gonna be on the soccer team. She was recruited and everything. Don't know where she gets it. Not from me. It's funny how kids just latch on to these things and *go*. Like your boy with his birds maybe.

VERONICA: Well, who knows how long that'll last.

Before birds it was old airplanes, like from World War Two. He gets a new obsession every two weeks seems like. He's always onto the next thing so fast, it's hard for me to keep up.

HOGAN: He got a father?

(*Beat.*)

VERONICA: Yes.

Both of my children do, actually.

HOGAN: Oh hey. I didn't mean to, uh—

VERONICA: And the father of both of my children passed away, two years ago. All right?

HOGAN: Oh jeez.

Sorry.

VERONICA: Thank you.

(*Beat.*)

HOGAN: How?

VERONICA: Hit and run. On the street in front of our building.

HOGAN: Well shit.

(*Beat.*)

VERONICA: Excuse me, I'm going to bring the children their lunch.

(*She exits.*)

HOGAN: I'll see what I can do about the water heater.

Fade.

SCENE 3

That evening. VERONICA *alone. She looks troubled. She tries to settle down to read a paperback. Her cell phone rings.*

VERONICA: Charles? Hi, thanks for calling me back. I'm fine. We're— Yes, everything is fine but I needed to tell you something, you'll probably hear it from Mia. There was a little incident today out on the lake. It— No, everything's fine, but she— Charles? Can you hear me? Charles?

Sorry, is this better? I'm just losing you a little up here. Is that any better? Charles—? Shit.

(She moves to a different part of the room. Cell phone rings.)

Hi. I'm sorry. The service up here— Yes, okay. Well, look, all it was was Mia was out swimming with my kids and she got out a little far and must have got a mouthful of water. Excuse me? No. No. I was out there with them, right on the shore. No, I wasn't swimming, I was just watching them and I— Charles. Charles. I'm gonna tell you the whole story, all right? Just hold on. She got out a little far and got a mouthful of water and went under a second so I jumped in and pulled her out, the whole thing wasn't more than maybe ten seconds and everything was fine after, I gave them all hot chocolate and everybody's good but I just wanted you to hear it from me right away. I don't think so. No, you don't have to come up. She's having a great time. Uh-huh.

(HOGAN *knocks and enters. He carries a carton of eggs.*)

Well, you did say she had passed her Red Cross test. Well, actually she wasn't even out farther than she could stand, it was just one of those things where she opened her mouth at the wrong time and got a faceful of water and then got scared, it could've happened in the bathtub. I know, she swims better than my kids. She's asleep now. Ate a big supper, uh-huh. Hot dogs and baked beans. No, I got her the tofu dogs. Yeah, I'll have her call you first thing. What? You're cutting out. Hello——? I'll have her call you first thing in the morning——

(*She hangs up.*)

Asshole.

HOGAN: Uh-oh. Salty language!

(*Beat.*)

You need to call him back?

VERONICA: What? No.

HOGAN: He wasn't mad, was he?

VERONICA: Sorry, do you want to tell me what you're doing back here?

HOGAN: Just making sure everything's okay.

VERONICA: Everything is fine.

HOGAN: The water heater——

VERONICA: It's fine! It was fine at four o'clock when you got done fixing it.

HOGAN: Just because it was running before doesn't mean it stayed running long enough to heat up the tank. I thought you'd appreciate me coming back to check up on it.

And I brought you some eggs.

(*He goes to put them in the fridge.*)

VERONICA: Eggs?

HOGAN: From my brother's.

VERONICA: What, does he keep chickens or something?

HOGAN: No.

(*Beat.*)

VERONICA: I see you found some dry clothes.

HOGAN: Yeah.

VERONICA: Good thing you didn't clear out those drawers like you said, you got plenty of extra clothes around the place.

(*She gets settled again on the couch.*)

HOGAN: What are you reading?

VERONICA: Mystery.

HOGAN: Any good?

VERONICA: Yeah, I'd like to finish it.

(*Beat.*)

HOGAN: He wasn't blaming you, was he? The dad.

VERONICA: He was just concerned.

HOGAN: Why'd you say "asshole" then?

VERONICA: I didn't.

HOGAN: Yeah you did.

VERONICA: Oh whatever, he was just worried about his little girl.

HOGAN: He wanted to come get her?

VERONICA: What difference does it make?

HOGAN: You think he doesn't trust you?

VERONICA: I don't care if he trusts me or not.

HOGAN: Seems like you do.

VERONICA: He trusts me, he let me take his girl for the week. He's just one of those parents, you know, one of *those* parents.

HOGAN: What kind?

VERONICA: You know.

HOGAN: White?

VERONICA: What? No.

HOGAN: Sorry.

VERONICA: I mean, yes he is, but that's not what I mean.

HOGAN: Uh-huh.

VERONICA: I mean that kind of New York parent like, oh she got a nut allergy so if you have even one almond anywhere in the house it's an emergency.

And makes his kid wear a helmet all the time. Pushing her on a swing at the playground. Like she's going skydiving.

HOGAN: Really? On a swing?

VERONICA: Maybe not that. But like that.

HOGAN: You were making peanut butter sandwiches earlier.

VERONICA: I gave her plain jelly! She ain't gonna go into anaphylactic shock looking at the Skippy jar. And guess what? If she does I got an EpiPen. I've got everything. I could perform open-heart surgery with the kit I brought up here. I'm equipped. So don't go and sort of imply that . . .

HOGAN: That what?

VERONICA: Whatever. It doesn't matter.

Oh and by the way. Something else you forgot to clear out your drawers before we got here, your magazines. My little boy found them. I put them in a bag by the door, you can take them when you go.

HOGAN: What's the big deal? So I left some hunting and fishing magazines—

VERONICA: It wasn't just hunting and fishing. You left something else mixed in there.

HOGAN: Oh.

VERONICA: Yeah, oh. So tonight I got a seven-year-old showing me—

HOGAN: Yeah, okay, that is my fault.

VERONICA: Thanks a lot.

HOGAN: That is a little embarrassing, I'm sorry about that.

VERONICA: You should be.

HOGAN: Oh come on, it's not *so* strange.

You're a nurse.

VERONICA: What does that mean?

(HOGAN *shrugs.*)

All right. If you don't mind, I'm gonna read my book and then I'm gonna go to bed so good *night*, for heaven's sake.

HOGAN: Okay. I'll be out in the truck if you need anything.

(*He starts to go.*)

VERONICA: Wait.

HOGAN: What?

VERONICA: Out in the *truck*?

HOGAN: Way down the drive. Near the road. You can't see it from here.

VERONICA: Is that where you've been while you were waiting to check the water heater? Sitting in your truck the whole time?

HOGAN: Sort of.

VERONICA: What do you mean, "sort of"?

HOGAN: Well, since it's come up . . . I've sort of been sleeping out there.

(*Beat. She stares at him.*)

VERONICA: What?

HOGAN: Debbie kicked me out.

VERONICA: Who?

HOGAN: My sister-in-law. The attorney? I mean, she didn't so much kick me out as make it clear she didn't want me staying there at all while you were renting. And my brother's too pussy-whipped to say no. Can you believe that? My little brother.

VERONICA: How long have you been out there?

HOGAN: I guess more or less since you arrived.

VERONICA: Oh my God.

HOGAN: Did you know I was there?

VERONICA: No, I didn't know you were there!

HOGAN: So what's the problem?

VERONICA: I'm *renting* this place! Do you understand that? *I am renting this property.* You are not supposed to be *on* the property.

HOGAN: Come on, I'm *barely* on the property.

VERONICA: No. I am sick of this. This is bullshit.

HOGAN: What?

VERONICA: This is one of the biggest mistakes I ever made.

Renting this rat-hole, and you skulking around the property like some weird freak—I'm sorry but that's what you are, you are freaking me out! I am done with this.

HOGAN: What do you mean?

VERONICA: I am done. We are leaving.

HOGAN: The kids are sleeping.

VERONICA: First thing in the morning. Right now I want you out of here. Go. Park your truck *elsewhere*. Do you understand me?

HOGAN: You're acting like I'm dangerous or something.

VERONICA: I will call the police. I swear I will call 911.

HOGAN: You think *I'm* dangerous? You're lucky I was around here today!

VERONICA: Yeah, 'cause you were skulking around like the creepy oddball you are.

HOGAN: I wasn't—

VERONICA: Creepy backwoods oddball freak.

HOGAN: You should be thanking me!

VERONICA: Oh, just shut up and get out of here, will you, please? We'll be gone in the morning. Then you can move back into this dump, with your hockey sticks and sleazy magazines—

HOGAN: You're the dangerous one.

VERONICA: Excuse me?

HOGAN: Kids who can barely swim—yeah, I watched them, they're not as good as you think they are—leaving those kids all by themselves in the water while you're off God knows where.

VERONICA: No. Don't you dare suggest—

HOGAN: And it's pretty convenient, isn't it? This threat to leave. Given that you still owe me a third of the rent.

VERONICA: It's not a threat and you ain't never getting that money. Ever! This whole deal is *over*. And my kids are good swimmers! I taught them myself! This is over now. Will you just get out of here now, Hogan? *Now?*

HOGAN: Where did you go anyway?

VERONICA: What?

HOGAN: While the kids were swimming.

VERONICA: Nowhere.

HOGAN: You weren't in the house.

VERONICA: I got a phone call. It was important. I had to walk down the road to get a decent signal. I told them to come up on the beach—

HOGAN: You should have just asked me. I would've stopped work, watched the kids.

VERONICA: Look, what do you want? You want me to thank you again?

HOGAN: You never thanked me the first time. After I jumped in the lake, saved a drowning child.

VERONICA: I was right there the second I heard her yell!

HOGAN: After you heard her yell maybe the third or fourth time.

VERONICA: Third time, first time, who cares?

HOGAN: Well, I was already there pulling her out and you just seem pissed off about it.

VERONICA: I'm not.

HOGAN: You sure have been acting pissed off about it.

VERONICA: Sorry.

I—I'm glad you helped me out. I am. But I was just down the road within earshot and three more seconds I would have waded in and grabbed her wrist just like you did only you beat me to it.

HOGAN: Little girl drowning and you make a phone call.

VERONICA: Oh for God's sake she wasn't *drowning*, she—

(*The phone rings.* VERONICA *jumps.*)

Jesus.

HOGAN: I thought you said it was disconnected.

VERONICA: It was. It hasn't worked all week.

(*It keeps ringing.*)

HOGAN: Maybe you should get that?

VERONICA: Why?

HOGAN: She's gonna let it ring until somebody picks up.

VERONICA: Who?

HOGAN: Debbie.

Please? Just see what she wants? I can't deal with her.

VERONICA: That's your problem.

HOGAN: She knows I'm here. She's done this before. That phone's gonna keep ringing.

VERONICA: So answer it.

HOGAN: Uh-uh. No way.

VERONICA: Hogan. Pick up the phone.

HOGAN: No.

VERONICA: It's gonna wake the kids.

HOGAN: Yeah, I know, so you better pick it up.

VERONICA: It's your phone. Pick up the goddamn phone.

HOGAN: No.

(*It keeps ringing.*)

VERONICA: Jesus.

(VERONICA *goes to the phone, furious, and picks it up.*)

What.

Yes, I am the renter. Who is this?

Well, you can tell me your name too. Uh-huh.

Well, my name is Veronica Barnes. B-A-R-N-E-S.

That's right.

Because he rented to me.

No, we are not "friends."

On the *Internet.*

Well, you're gonna have to talk to him about that.

(HOGAN *gestures "I'm not here."*)

Again, those are issues you will have to take up with your brother-in-law.

He's—

(VERONICA *looks at* HOGAN, *who makes pleading gestures. Beat.*)

No. He's not here right now. Why would he be? It's nine o'clock at night. I don't know where he is.

Uh-huh. All right. I don't have a piece of paper. Okay . . .

(*A pause as she listens.*)

I see. Okay. I will. Goodbye.

(*She hangs up.*)

HOGAN: Thanks.

You didn't have to do that.

(*Beat.*)

VERONICA: She was rude.

HOGAN: I told you.

What was she saying?

VERONICA: That you need to call her. Something about a compromise. That the homeowners' association—something, they're willing to drop the complaint, but you got to vacate the property.

HOGAN: What?

VERONICA: That's what she said.

HOGAN: Oh, that is just bullshit. Who said she could even negotiate on my behalf? She never formally agreed to represent me. *Vacate the property?* What does that even mean?

VERONICA: It sounds pretty obvious.

HOGAN: It's bullshit! It's a blatant conflict of interest! My brother and I *co-own* the property. It was left to us *jointly*. So she comes along and negotiates a "compromise" that just happens to produce the outcome she's wanted all these years, which is to get the place all to herself? It's ridiculous! It'll never stand up in a court of law. I'll appeal. I'll appeal this all the way to the Supreme Court if I have to.

VERONICA: What are you talking about? You're not even *in* court.

HOGAN: *Vacate*. She is just completely out of control.

VERONICA: Maybe if you asked her before you rented she wouldn't be so upset.

HOGAN: I don't have to ask her permission.

VERONICA: Maybe you do. If you co-own the place. And they pay the utilities—she must have paid the phone bill. And you didn't even ask them before you put it online. You didn't even tell them until a few days ago.

HOGAN: She told you that?

VERONICA: Yes.

HOGAN: Why are you on her side all of a sudden?

VERONICA: I ain't on anybody's side. But it seems like maybe she's got a point. Especially if you're keeping all the rental money for yourself.

HOGAN: What? She told you *that*, too?

VERONICA: No. That I just figured.

(*Beat.*)

HOGAN: Look, here's the thing. She comes here—they all come here to use the lake in the summer, right? Her and my brother and their kids. I have my own kid I'd like to bring up here! But I can't, right? I *can't*, and they act like they're the only one with any right to it. They just show up whenever they want. Sometimes they want to have cookouts with other families. Parties . . . The girls—they got twin girls, my nieces—they both drive now, they show up on their own, bring their boyfriends— I'm *living* here.

VERONICA: So don't live here.

HOGAN: *Where the hell am I supposed to go?*

VERONICA: How do I know? God, I'm sick of listening to you complain. I got problems of my own.

HOGAN: Oh, boo-fuckin'-hoo.

VERONICA: You don't even know.

HOGAN: At least you got your kids *with* you, you know? Count your fucking blessings. And a fancy *job*—

VERONICA: I lost my job.

(*Beat.*)

HOGAN: The nursing job?

VERONICA: Yes.

HOGAN: When?

VERONICA: Week before I came up here.

(*Beat.*)

HOGAN: That why you never paid me the last third of the rent?

(**VERONICA** *makes a dismissive gesture.*)

You should have just told me.

(*Beat.*)

Look, it happens.

VERONICA: Not to me.

HOGAN: It's happened to me maybe twenty, thirty times.

VERONICA: Yeah, well, you're a loser.

(*Beat.*)

HOGAN: You didn't have to say that.

VERONICA: Sorry.

HOGAN: Not just losers who get laid off.

VERONICA: I didn't just get laid off.

HOGAN: You got fired?

(*She makes a "bingo" gesture.*)

Still doesn't mean it was your fault.

VERONICA: Oh, it was, there's no doubt about that.

HOGAN: Come on.

VERONICA: It was.

HOGAN: What'd you do, poison somebody? Give 'em the wrong injection?

VERONICA: No.

HOGAN: What?

VERONICA: It doesn't matter.

HOGAN: Did you—

VERONICA: *I really don't want to talk about this anymore, if you don't mind.*

(*She sits down, visibly upset. Beat.*)

HOGAN: Look. Finish the week.

I'll stay out of the way. I'll go in town during the day and at night I'll park at the far end of the property and be gone again at daybreak, you won't see or hear me. I'll clear up all the stuff with my family, it won't affect you.

Those kids are having a good time. You don't want to disappoint them and you don't want a hassle from that girl's dad for bringing her back early. You don't want to waste your car rental. And the weather's supposed to be terrific next few days. I'll even spring for the inner tubes. Okay? Now, you're never gonna get a better deal than that.

(*He puts out his hand. Beat. Then* VERONICA *reluctantly takes it.*)

All right.

(*He starts to go.*)

VERONICA: Hogan.

(*He stops.*)

Thank you. For the girl.

HOGAN: Anytime.

(*Beat.*)

VERONICA: Can I ask you something?

HOGAN: Sure.

VERONICA: Why can't you bring your daughter up here?

(*Beat.*)

HOGAN: I sent her an e-mail back in May.

"Guess what? I'm finally building that diving platform. It'll be ready this summer. You can come up and visit." This is before I even knew she'd be going to school an hour away.

"You can swim. The cabin's still here. The lake's the same as it ever was. Everything's the same."

It bounced back. She changed her e-mail. I called her mother to get the new one. She said, in this voice, this very *precise* voice, she said she was asked, by our daughter, not to give it to me; and she felt she should respect our daughter's preference. (*Shrugs.*) Well, that's her preference. (*He exits.*)

Fade.

SCENE 4

Night. VERONICA *is bagging surplus groceries. She starts to fold a pile of kids' clothes. She stops for a moment, listening to the night. It's quiet.*

Beat.

The sound of a truck. Headlights in the window. Motor turns off. Truck door opens and closes. Lights stay on.

VERONICA: Hogan?

HOGAN: (*Off.*) Yep.

VERONICA: Turn those lights off.

HOGAN: Oh.

(*The lights go off.* HOGAN *enters. A bottle of Old Grand-Dad. He looks a little unsteady.*)

Told you I'd stay away.

VERONICA: Uh-huh.

(*Beat.*)

HOGAN: Getting ready to go?

VERONICA: Yes.

HOGAN: Tomorrow morning.

VERONICA: Yep.

HOGAN: How were your last days? Was I right about the weather or what?

VERONICA: They were real nice.

(*Beat.*)

HOGAN: Just thought I'd check to see if you needed anything else before you go.

VERONICA: No, I think we're okay, thanks.

Oh. One of my kids broke a cereal bowl. You tell me how much it costs and I'll pay for it.

HOGAN: That's all right.

VERONICA: No, take it out of the damage deposit. I don't want to—

HOGAN: It's just a bowl. Forget it.

(*Beat.*)

Did we end up doing the damage deposit?

VERONICA: Yeah, in the first two payments, remember?

HOGAN: Right, yes.

Oh—but the third payment never—

VERONICA: We said we'd forget about all that.

HOGAN: Right, right, right right right.

VERONICA: Let's not go through this again, please. I've had a real nice couple days—

HOGAN: Of course. No.

(*Beat.*)

VERONICA: So you still have to return my damage deposit.

HOGAN: Yes. Absolutely. I'll do a quick walk-through tomorrow, then send it off first thing.

(*Beat.*)

VERONICA: Oh, I dropped a coffee mug, too. I tried to glue it but it wouldn't glue so I threw it out.

HOGAN: Don't worry about it.

Unless it was my 1980 Lake Placid Miracle on Ice mug.

VERONICA: I think it was, yeah.

HOGAN: Shit.

VERONICA: I'll pay for it.

HOGAN: That was a collector's item. There's no way you can afford to replace it. If you could even find a replacement.

VERONICA: Well, you shouldn't have left it here if it was so valuable.

HOGAN: I didn't think you'd *use* it.

VERONICA: Why wouldn't I use it? It's a coffee mug.

HOGAN: It's clearly a collector's item.

VERONICA: Then you shouldn't have left it on the shelf with the other cups.

If it's so important to you—

HOGAN: Never mind, just forget it.

VERONICA: I'll pay for it.

HOGAN: *Forget it, I said.*

VERONICA: I'm sorry.

(*Beat.*)

HOGAN: So I brought you something. Little farewell gift.

(*He gives her a wrapped present.*)

Just to sort of say no hard feelings kind of thing.

VERONICA: Oh. Well, thank you.

HOGAN: Open it.

(*She does. It's a book.*)

VERONICA: *A Child's First Book of Birds.*

HOGAN: See, I saw this and I thought *this* would be the one for a seven-year-old. See, it's got pop-up pages? And you can pull that flap and make the wings beat, there's a bunch of stuff like that, and check this out:

(*He presses a button and the book emits a birdcall.*)

For each one you can hear the actual call. That's pretty incredible, huh? Tiny little speaker in there somehow. So your boy can really learn them now.

VERONICA: That's—thank you very much. That's very . . .

HOGAN: Of course you're leaving. But there's birds in the city, too, right?

VERONICA: Yeah.

HOGAN: There's an inscription.

(*She flips to it, reads.*)

VERONICA: "To Veronica, with affection and respect, Terry Hogan."

HOGAN: Of course, it's really for your son, but I didn't know his name.

VERONICA: I'm really . . . thank you, Hogan. I don't know what to say.

HOGAN: Okay then.

(*He starts to go. Stops.*)

Oh. Uh. Earlier today . . .

VERONICA: Yeah?

HOGAN: I guess around dinnertime I saw—I saw a car pull in here. I wasn't watching the place or anything. I was just parked in the woods off the road in and I happened to notice—

VERONICA: It was your brother.

HOGAN: Shit. I thought so. Did he give you a hard time?

VERONICA: No. He was perfectly nice. Apologized for everything. I said there was nothing to apologize for.

HOGAN: Oh, well, that's good.

VERONICA: He was looking for you.

Maybe you oughta talk to him.

HOGAN: Where'd you say I'd gone?

VERONICA: Nowhere. I didn't know where you went to. I was just glad I had one day here with everything working for once.

(*Beat.*)

He knows you're hiding from him.

HOGAN: I wasn't hiding from him.

VERONICA: Whatever, avoiding him.

HOGAN: I just went to get something to drink.

VERONICA: Well, it looks like you succeeded.

Now, maybe you should go now, finish your drink in your truck.

HOGAN: You really don't think much of me, do you?

I'm not gonna sit and just guzzle this down alone in the woods in my truck. I use a glass.

VERONICA: Okay.

HOGAN: Can I borrow a glass?

VERONICA: It's your cabin.

(*He goes, gets a glass, returns.*)

HOGAN: You want some?

VERONICA: No.

(*Beat.*)

HOGAN: Okay then. I guess that's it. I won't be around here in the morning, so good luck and take care and all that.

(*He starts to go.*)

VERONICA: Hogan.

   You should give that money back.

HOGAN: What money?

VERONICA: The money your brother said you took from them.

HOGAN: What?

VERONICA: You heard me.

HOGAN: It's bullshit.

VERONICA: Uh-huh.

HOGAN: It's Debbie. She makes up these accusations. She hates me. You know, you've talked to her.

VERONICA: He said it was a lot. Like five thousand dollars?

HOGAN: (*Dismissive sound.*)

VERONICA: That sounds serious to me.

HOGAN: It isn't true!

VERONICA: It's not my problem either way. But it sounds like something you better work out.

HOGAN: I will.

VERONICA: Okay.

(*Beat.*)

HOGAN: It's not true, though. My brother, he's basically a good kid. We used to be close before he got married. It's her. She poisons him. It's sad is what it is.

VERONICA: You got a record already. Don't be stupid.

HOGAN: I don't have a record. Is that what he told you?

(*She looks at him.*)

It wasn't anything *bad*. Jeez. Don't look at me like that.

VERONICA: What was it?

(*Beat.*)

HOGAN: Check-kiting.

VERONICA: What's that?

HOGAN: Writing bad checks, basically.

VERONICA: You do it?

HOGAN: I guess I did. I mean, they proved it in court. It wasn't exactly intentional. I'm not some criminal mastermind. I have trouble keeping track of my net worth sometimes. It was more sloppiness than anything else.

VERONICA: How long were you . . .

HOGAN: Fourteen months. You know, *that's* probably the thing with my brother. He's like me: bad at keeping track of stuff, a little disorganized, never balances his checkbook . . . Debbie probably noticed some kind of problem with their checking account or something, some little discrepancy, and in her mind, Oh, we're a little short this month, plus convicted check-kiting brother-in-law I've never liked, *therefore inevitably equals* . . . she jumps to the obvious, or should I say most convenient, conclusion. I bet you anything that's what's going on here. Yeah?

VERONICA: Sure, maybe.

HOGAN: *Maybe?*

I would never. Not from my own *family*.

VERONICA: Okay.

HOGAN: You don't believe me.

(Beat. She looks away.)

Fine. Don't believe me, then. I don't give a shit . . .

(He grabs his glass and starts to go. The glass slips out of his hand and breaks.)

Goddamn it.

VERONICA: It's all right, I got it.

(*He tries to clean it up.*)

HOGAN: Ow. Shit.

VERONICA: What happened? You cut your hand?

HOGAN: It's fine.

VERONICA: Stop. You're bleeding.

HOGAN: I'm okay. Never mind.

VERONICA: You got a big piece of glass sticking out of your hand. Let me look at that.

HOGAN: Leave me alone. Don't worry about it.

VERONICA: Let me do this. Hold still, you idiot.

(*She removes the glass.*)

HOGAN: Ow!

VERONICA: Hush. Just stay there.

(*She exits. He holds his T-shirt against his bloody hand. She returns with her bag.*)

Come here. Sit down. Sit *down*, I said.

(*He sits. She starts to treat and bandage his hand.*)

Your hands ain't too clean.

You ain't too clean. When's the last time you did your laundry?

HOGAN: Maybe I should just go outside, jump in the water.

VERONICA: Nah, you don't want to do that. It's getting chilly.

Just maybe get yourself a shower and change your clothes, you been sleeping in that truck too much. That truck doesn't look too clean either. I'll let you take a shower here if you need to.

(*Beat.*)

HOGAN: You must really think I'm a piece of shit, huh?

(*Beat.*)

VERONICA: At least you rented to me.

HOGAN: You were the only one responded to the ad.

VERONICA: Well, this wasn't the only house I looked at. I came up the week before and saw another place nicer. A lot nicer. But the sweet old lady who owned it took a look at me coming up the driveway and said, You're too late, dear, it's just been rented.

HOGAN: You gotta expect that kind of thing, I guess.

VERONICA: I expected it from you. I nearly got right back on the bus when I saw you the first time.

(*She finishes.*)

Better?

HOGAN: Yeah. You're very good.

VERONICA: Well, thank you very much.

(*She cleans up the broken glass.*)

I sewed a man's finger back on once. Whole tip of his finger. His knife slipped chopping lettuce, he said. There were no doctors around, I put it back on for him. Fifteen minutes. He walked out of there, went back to his restaurant where he worked or wherever. I thought, I just put a man's finger back on his hand.

(*She throws out the glass. She returns.*)

HOGAN: Why'd they fire you?

(*Beat.*)

VERONICA: I wasn't what I said I was.

HOGAN: What are you?

VERONICA: I'm a nurse.

HOGAN: That's what you said you were.

VERONICA: I said I was a nurse practitioner.

HOGAN: Oh yeah.

I'm still not that clear on the difference, to be honest.

VERONICA: Well there's like a thirty-thousand-dollar-a-year difference.

HOGAN: Okay, that I get.

So you exaggerated a little bit, I don't care.

VERONICA: The *hospital* cared.

(*Beat.*)

HOGAN: Oh. You told *them*—

VERONICA: You know, you're like Sherlock Holmes. You're a fuckin' genius.

HOGAN: Sorry.

(*Beat.*)

VERONICA: When my husband passed I'd done all the work for that degree except one year.

The summer after he died I'd take the kids out sometimes to the beach or someplace? But that's just for the day. And it's a long day, and everybody gets cranky, you're all exhausted and sandy on the train coming home, and the kids start fighting, and then you're just back in your apartment and somebody's got to make dinner . . . It's almost worse than when you left that morning. It's like you never went anywhere.

So when I saw that hospital job opened up . . . that perfect job I knew I could do as well as anybody . . . probably *better* . . .

HOGAN: You tweaked your résumé a little bit.

VERONICA: I submitted a false *transcript*. I *lied* about my *credentials*.

HOGAN: Huh.

(*Beat.*)

It's actually pretty impressive.

(*She glares.*)

I mean, to pull that off.

VERONICA: I didn't pull it off, that's the point!

HOGAN: You did for a while. How'd you get caught?

VERONICA: Another nurse in my department wrote a few too many prescriptions for her "friends." After she got arrested they went and did an extra background check on everybody.

HOGAN: And they spotted your little creative whatever.

VERONICA: Now I'm probably even gonna lose my regular RN license. I have to go before a review board. I had to beg to get to do *that*.

  That's why they called. The other day. That's why I had to walk down the road. To beg for a chance to beg the board to keep my license.

(*Beat.*)

HOGAN: Well, I can see why you had to walk down the road to deal with that.

VERONICA: I still can't believe I left the kids swimming, I felt so bad afterward I wanted to . . .

(*Beat.*)

So I don't think you're a—what you said. But listen. If you made a mistake, and there's any way to correct it . . . you should really try and correct it.

HOGAN: I didn't take their damn money!

VERONICA: Hogan.

HOGAN: What do I have to do to convince you?

VERONICA: I'm just trying to help you is all.

HOGAN: Sounds like you're the one who needs help. Just 'cause you're walking around with a guilty conscience doesn't mean you have to start lecturing me—

VERONICA: All right, forget I said anything.

HOGAN: I mean it's my *family*, for God's sake.

VERONICA: All right! I'm sorry. Okay?

HOGAN: Okay.

(*Beat.*)

Anyway, back to your thing. Here's my opinion:

VERONICA: I didn't ask for your—

HOGAN: I really don't think you should blame yourself. Okay yes, you screwed up. But it could have been a lot worse.

VERONICA: How?

HOGAN: Did you say you knew how to do something you didn't know how to do, kill a patient or something?

VERONICA: No.

HOGAN: All right. So that's a major plus right there. That's huge.

And you probably really needed to, right? Or you wouldn't have done it. You *almost* had the degree, right? The last year of school was probably bullshit anyway, just papers and exams and stuff, you want to move things along, you roll the dice a little bit. That's completely understandable! I mean it wasn't very intelligent but it's understandable. Plus with the whole dead husband thing, I mean come on!

And you're a good mother, hell, you're a *great* mother. You want to take good care of your kids. You want to be able to give them nice vacations, get them swimming in a goddamn lake in the sunshine instead of indoors for once. Don't beat yourself up about it.

VERONICA: No?

HOGAN: No. You'll be all right. Don't worry. It's all gonna work out, you'll see.

VERONICA: Maybe. Maybe it won't.

HOGAN: Well, you know what they say. Bad luck runs in streaks. You know, one domino falls and then another one and then another one and another one. Bip, bip, bip, bip, bip. But eventually they have to stop, right?

(*Beat.*)

You know, when I got divorced—

VERONICA: I really don't want to hear it.

HOGAN: Okay.

(*Beat.*)

You want to go outside, shoot at some stuff?

(*She stares at him.*)

I've got a rifle in the truck. We can set up some bottles and cans on the road, blow off steam. I do it when I'm fed up sometimes. It's surprisingly relaxing.

(*Beat.*)

VERONICA: You know, I think I would really enjoy that right now.

HOGAN: Really?

VERONICA: You know what would make it even more fun?

HOGAN: What?

VERONICA: Blindfolds.

(*He stares at her.*)

HOGAN: You're messing with me.

(*She laughs.*)

Okay.

(*Beat.*)

What are you going to do? When you go back.

VERONICA: I don't know. I don't know what's going to happen.

(*Beat. He drinks. He tentatively puts a hand on her thigh.*)

You're kidding, right?

(*He removes it.*)

HOGAN: Right.

I'd better go.

(*He gets up, goes to the door.*)

VERONICA: What are *you* gonna do? After we leave?

HOGAN: No real plans.

I'll manage.

He waves, exits, goes out to the truck.

The motor starts. Lights shine into the cabin for a moment, then swing away. It's dark again and quiet.

Beat.

She picks up the bird book. She presses one of the buttons. A birdcall. She presses it again.

Fade.

SCENE 5

January. The cabin looks uninhabited. Bottles, other rubbish. VERONICA *appears outside. She knocks. No answer. Tentatively comes in. She has a couple of take-out bags.*

VERONICA: Hogan? Hogan?

(*She looks around. She sets the bags down. While her back is turned* HOGAN *enters, bleary.*)

HOGAN: I heard your voice. I thought I was dreaming.

VERONICA: I knocked. You didn't answer.

HOGAN: I was napping.

(*Beat.*)

VERONICA: I brought you some coffee.

HOGAN: I don't drink coffee. I'm a tea drinker.

VERONICA: Oh.

(*Tentative.*) Well, there's some doughnuts too. And I got a couple butter rolls, in case you're hungry. And a fruit salad.

HOGAN: A fruit salad?

VERONICA: Yes. Are you hungry at all?

HOGAN: What are you doing here?

VERONICA: I have a . . .

> (*Resets.*) I came to see how you were doing.

HOGAN: I'm fine.

VERONICA: You want me to put that heater on?

HOGAN: It's broken. I've been meaning to replace it.

VERONICA: You don't look fine.

HOGAN: You woke me up. What do you want?

VERONICA: Look, I'm not sure how to . . .

(*Beat.*)

I got your envelope.

(*He says nothing. She digs in her handbag.*)

I got this envelope sent to my house. Did you send it? I haven't seen you or talked to you for six months and this comes, no return address, no note, just cash. Forty-five hundred dollars cash money. Sent through the mail.

HOGAN: So?

VERONICA: Did you send it?

HOGAN: Yes.

VERONICA: Why?

HOGAN: I thought you could use it. Given your situation.

(*Beat.*)

VERONICA: I called here. The phone is, once again, disconnected. I called your brother—

HOGAN: Oh jeez, why?

VERONICA: Because I'm looking for you to find out what's going on with this!

HOGAN: You didn't tell them—

VERONICA: I just asked to speak with you.

HOGAN: I don't know why you went to all the trouble. That's what the money was for, to make things a little easier.

VERONICA: You really thought I'd keep it?

HOGAN: Why not?

VERONICA: It's the money you took from your brother.

HOGAN: Not all of it. I kept five hundred for myself.

VERONICA: It's stolen.

HOGAN: No, it's *missing*. The only way they'd know it was stolen was if you showed up on their doorstep like an idiot and tried to give it back to them.

VERONICA: I didn't try to give it back. I only talked to them on the phone. We didn't discuss it at all.

HOGAN: Good. Keep it.

VERONICA: You know I can't.

(*She sets it down.*)

HOGAN: You find another job?

VERONICA: Not yet.

HOGAN: So don't you need it? What about your kids?

VERONICA: They're—we're getting a little help right now.

HOGAN: From who?

VERONICA: Hogan. Just listen to me and let me do this. All right? Your brother said they've been trying to reach you but you won't talk to them.

He said he's driven out here and you won't come to the door.

HOGAN: I probably wasn't home.

VERONICA: He said one time you pulled a gun on him.

HOGAN: Oh, that is ridiculous.

VERONICA: He said you came to the door with your shotgun.

HOGAN: I don't have a shotgun. I have a rifle.

VERONICA: Whatever.

HOGAN: There's a difference. He should know that. It belonged to our dad. It's a 1940s Remington. It's a collector's item. I might have been holding it when I came out but it's just because he was pounding on the door saying he was gonna kick it in.

VERONICA: All right, whatever. I don't care about that. The point is they're worried about you.

HOGAN: Right.

VERONICA: They are. You think I wanted to get involved with this? I wouldn't be up here if they hadn't begged me to give you a message.

HOGAN: Why you?

VERONICA: He said there isn't anybody else. Your wife didn't want to get involved, and your daughter just started—

HOGAN: All right, never mind.

VERONICA: Your daughter just started school, they don't want her upset—

HOGAN: *I don't want anybody talking to my daughter.*

VERONICA: They know that! That's why when I called they asked me—

HOGAN: Why the hell did they think I'd listen to you?

VERONICA: That's what I said. He said, You're his friend, aren't you?

HOGAN: What'd you say?

VERONICA: No, not exactly. But I said I'd try.

HOGAN: Try what?

(*Beat.*)

VERONICA: You can go back there, they said. They—just hear me out now. They asked me to tell you that they'll take you in. At least for a while. Let bygones be bygones. Till you can get things sorted out a little bit. Debbie agrees.

HOGAN: You've got to be kidding me.

VERONICA: It was her idea, I think. It sounded like she talked your brother into it. She told me. She said, Please try to convince him.

HOGAN: Debbie said that.

VERONICA: Yes.

HOGAN: That's why you came all the way up here? To deliver this "message"?

VERONICA: Well, like I said, they were very concerned.

HOGAN: (*Dismissive sound.*)

VERONICA: I'll tell you what. I'll drive over there with you tonight if you want. Help you pack up whatever you need here. If there is anything. You shouldn't be staying here now anyway, it's freezing.

HOGAN: It's fine once you get the heater on.

VERONICA: The heater's *broken*, you said.

I can't be here all night, Hogan. I'd like to get home and put my kids to bed.

Maybe just let me take you over there so you can talk to them yourself?

HOGAN: I got nothing to say to them.

VERONICA: What would it hurt to stay a couple nights?

HOGAN: If you think I'm leaving here you're crazy.

VERONICA: Just till you can get yourself together a little bit.

HOGAN: I don't need to get myself together!

VERONICA: Look *around*.

HOGAN: No. You don't—somehow you have got the wrong idea here. I'm fine, all right? I'm perfectly fine. I know the place could use some straightening up, I've been meaning to get to that but I've been busy, and—you really didn't need to come up here. I don't need any help.

(*He picks up the cash.*)

For God's sake, I was trying to help *you*!

VERONICA: I don't want that kind of help.

HOGAN: (*Shouts.*) And I don't want your FUCKING SYMPATHY.

(*He throws the money at her. It flies everywhere.*)

WE'RE NOT FRIENDS. YOU DON'T KNOW ME. I WANT YOU OFF MY PROPERTY.

VERONICA: Oh what, are you gonna pull a gun on me now?

HOGAN: TRY ME.

VERONICA: GODDAMN IT, HOGAN, THEY SAID YOU NEARLY DIED.

(*Beat.*)

Debbie said—

HOGAN: (*Scorn.*) *Debbie.*

VERONICA: When they pulled you out of the lake.

HOGAN: She wasn't there. She doesn't know what she's talking about.

VERONICA: "Severe hypothermia." That's no joke. I've seen it.

HOGAN: That's an exaggeration.

VERONICA: That's a *coma*, Hogan. If whoever it was, that neighbor, hadn't seen you in the ice—

HOGAN: There was hardly any ice, the lake never freezes over anymore.

Look, I'm not saying it was a great situation or that I'm not grateful for the help, but you have to understand Debbie's agenda here. Bottom line, she would like to have me declared incompetent. You remember all that shit from last summer. Short of my actual death, that would be the best possible outcome for her. That would get her everything she wants.

VERONICA: I only talked to the woman a couple of times but she really didn't seem that bad, she—

HOGAN: She *hates* me. There is *nothing* she wouldn't say or do. She once ordered me—you are not going to believe this— to "stay the hell away" from her children! What is that? I don't have my own kid around—I'm missing her for chrissake!—if I offer to take my nieces to the movies or over to Putnam Lanes once in a while— Jesus Christ. This is the woman who accused me of stealing from her—

VERONICA: That was true.

HOGAN: That was a *fraction* of the money that I would have realized from the sale of this property—from which they were trying to have me vacated, remember? On the way to them taking the whole place for themselves. This is just one more excuse for them to get me out of their way—

VERONICA: How the hell did you end up in the lake, then?

(*Beat.*)

HOGAN: Well, that—

VERONICA: In January.

HOGAN: It was an accident.

VERONICA: What kind of an accident?

HOGAN: All right. I admit it sounds a little silly now.

I was trying to fix the dock.

VERONICA: In January?

HOGAN: I always felt bad about not fully completing that project. And I was out here . . .

I went through kind of I guess you'd call it a rough patch after last summer, you know, after you and your family had gone. I didn't stay here—it didn't seem wise, with all the tensions with my brother and sister-in-law, so there was a period there when I didn't have a firm base of operations, I was sort of floating more or less, you know, sleeping in the truck most nights. But I drove over here one day a couple weeks ago, gorgeous morning, just to check the place out, and it was so clear and sunny I just thought— there had been a little light snowfall the night before so even though the lake only had the thinnest skin of ice on the surface it *looked* thick, with the snow resting on it, it looked like it used to look when we were kids and we could skate after a big freeze.

VERONICA: You didn't—

HOGAN: What? No. I'm not an idiot. I knew I couldn't walk on it. I took the canoe. But it was such a gorgeous day—I don't know what it was like down in the city but up here it was gorgeous—I guess I just felt like this is the kind of day when you can do *anything*, you know. And maybe I was overambitious before, with the diving platform, but I've still got the lumber I bought, I can at least go out and replace some of the bad planks in the deck. It won't solve the pilings issue but maybe I can get us through another summer or two. I must have just slipped.

(*Beat.*)

VERONICA: I see.

HOGAN: The whole thing is sort of embarrassing in retrospect.

(*Beat. She's staring at him.*)

What?

VERONICA: They said . . . they found you in the water at night. Not the daytime. At night. And you were stripped down to your underwear, they said.

(*Beat.*)

HOGAN: (*Quietly.*) They would say that.

(*She takes a step toward him.*)

VERONICA: Please. You don't have to—

He backs away, knocking into a chair. Something snaps. He kicks the chair over. Knocks everything off a table. Smashes a lamp. A brief but destructive rampage. He stops, breathing hard.

He weeps. VERONICA *watches. A long beat.*

She goes, gets one of the bags. Takes out some napkins. Gives them to him.

Beat.

VERONICA: I'm gonna have one of those coffees before it gets too cold.

(*She takes a coffee. She sits. Sips it.*)

You sure you don't want a doughnut?

(*Beat.*)

HOGAN: What kind?

VERONICA: Glaze or plain.

HOGAN: Glaze.

VERONICA: Good, I like plain.

(*They eat. Long beat.*)

HOGAN: Who's with your kids?

VERONICA: What?

HOGAN: Who's taking care of your children?

VERONICA: Oh. Charles. Mia's father. My little girl's friend?

HOGAN: The helmet guy?

VERONICA: Turns out he's not so bad. I don't see why a ten-year-old needs to be a vegetarian, but whatever.

HOGAN: He the one helping you?

VERONICA: Yes.

(*Beat.*)

The board said no. The license board?

HOGAN: Oh yeah. Shit.

VERONICA: But Charles knows someone who places health-care providers with stay-at-home patients. It's not ideal. It's not like hospital work. But I can't be too picky right now. So that might work out, but it hasn't yet.

HOGAN: You sleeping with him?

VERONICA: What? Shut up.

HOGAN: Are you?

VERONICA: He's married.

(*Beat.*)

Separated.

(*Beat.*)

I don't know what we're doing.

HOGAN: Well. Congratulations.

VERONICA: I guess.

(*Beat.*)

HOGAN: You want to hear something funny?

VERONICA: God, yes.

HOGAN: I wasn't totally asleep when you drove up. I was kind of dozing. Kind of half asleep, I guess. That's why I was so confused to see you, I thought I might be dreaming. You know what I was thinking about?

VERONICA: No.

HOGAN: I was thinking about going down to the city sometime.

VERONICA: Yeah?

HOGAN: Yeah, I had this kind of fantasy, I guess you'd call it. (*She looks at him.*) It doesn't involve you, don't worry.

VERONICA: I'm not. That's not what I thought.

HOGAN: My daughter's at school there now, right? I was thinking about this the other day. What's to stop me getting in the truck and driving down?

I don't have her contact information but she's in one of the dorms someplace. How many dorms could there be? She's on a soccer scholarship. It shouldn't be that hard to find the playing fields. Anyway, I could track her down and take her to lunch.

(*Smiles.*) I've got the cash.

We could go someplace really upmarket. White table-cloth kind of thing. Actually, she's eighteen, she probably wouldn't want that. What do eighteen-year-olds like? I'd hate for it just to be pizza. Whatever, that doesn't matter. I picture just surprising her on the street outside her dorm as she's coming in from practice. Like she turns a corner and I'm standing there and she stops and I just say, Can I buy you lunch?

And maybe it would be a little awkward at first. I mean, of course it would be. Maybe she'd want to bring along a friend.

That would be fine, if it would make her more comfortable. A couple friends. The more the merrier, long as I'm buying.

You could even come. With your kids. I mean, we'd have to coordinate a little bit, I'm not sure how that fits in with the rest of it, the spontaneous part, but we could get a big round table someplace like a Chinese restaurant, with the dishes in the middle and one of those spinning disks, what are they called?

VERONICA: Lazy Susan.

HOGAN: Right. You can just turn it and everybody can help themselves to whatever they want.

VERONICA: That sounds good.

(*Beat.*)

HOGAN: I'm not going over there—

VERONICA: Just eat. We don't have to decide that right now.

HOGAN: Will you let me finish?

I'm not going over there with anybody thinking it wasn't an accident.

VERONICA: So it was an accident. We all have accidents.

(*Beat.*)

Okay. I'll tell you something funny too.

HOGAN: What?

VERONICA: My last night here? Back in August? I was packing up the kids' stuff, folding their clothes . . .

HOGAN: Yeah?

VERONICA: We had an okay couple days, you know, toward the end, and I was sitting there alone and it was nice and quiet for once, those damn crickets and frogs had shut up . . .

HOGAN: They do that when it's going to rain.

VERONICA: Really?

HOGAN: Yep.

VERONICA: How do they know?

HOGAN: I don't know. Air pressure maybe?

VERONICA: Huh.

Anyway. You know what I remember thinking? Even after everything that happened that week?

That I wish I could just stay here. In this shitty little cabin.

(*Beat. She laughs. He laughs too.*)

HOGAN: Well, we can't.

VERONICA: No.

Curtain.